ARCHITECTURE OF INDIA 2.0-3

I0483037

MR VIVEK KUMAR PANDEY
SHAMBHUNATH

Contents

1. Chapter 1   1

CHAPTER ONE

TOP 10 HISTORICAL MONUMENTS OF INDIA
HISTORICAL MONUMENTS
1. HAWA MAHAL

Hawa Mahal stands upright as the entrance to the City Palace, Jaipur. An important landmark in the city, Hawa Mahal is an epitome of the Rajputana architecture. The splendid five-storey "Palace of the Winds" is a blend of beauty and splendor much close to Rajasthan's culture. Maharaja Sawai Pratap Singh built Hawa Mahal in 1779. The pyramid shape of this ancient monument is a tourist attraction having 953 small windows.

2. TAJ MAHAL

Taj Mahal, the pinnacle of Mughal architecture, was built by the Mughal emperor Shah Jahan (1628-1658), grandson of Akbar the great, in the memory of his queen Arjumand Bano Begum, entitled 'Mumtaz Mahal'. Mumtaz Mahal was a niece of empress Nur Jahan and granddaughter of Mirza Ghias Beg I'timad-ud-Daula, wazir of emperor Jehangir. She was born in 1593 and died in 1631, during the birth of her fourteenth child at Burhanpur. Her mortal remains were temporarily buried in the Zainabad garden. Six months later, her body was transferred to Agra to be finally enshrined in the crypt of the main tomb of the Taj Mahal. The Taj Mahal is the mausoleum of both Mumtaz Mahal and

Shah Jahan.

3. MYSORE PALACE

The Mysore Palace, Karnataka is popularly known as the the Maharajah's Palace, situated at the city center at Mirza Road. Mysore Palace is one of the most fascinating monument of Mysore city. The other name of the Mysore Palace is Amba Vilas and is the largest palaces of India. Mysore's Wodeyar Mahararajas resided in the Mysore Palace of Karnataka.

The Mysore Palace is a three storied edifice with a length of 245 feet and breadth of 156 feet. The Mysore Palace at Karnataka comprises of a sequence of arched square towers enclosed by domes. The original palace of Mysore was carved out of wood which was accidentally burnt in 1897. The 24th Wodeyar Raja rebuilt the Mysore Palace of Karnataka in 1912. The Mysore Palace followed the Indo-Saracenic style of architecture.

4. VICTORIA MEMORIAL

Victoria Memorial, one of India's most beautiful monuments, represent a unique combination of classical European architecture and Mughal motifs. The domed and white marble museum sprawls over 64 acres and is set in a landscaped garden at the southern side of the Kolkata's maidan (ground) near Jawaharlal Nehru Road.

5. CHARMINAR

The charminar Hyderabad's best known landmark was built 1591 by Sultan Mohammed Quli Qutub Shah to appease the force of evil savaging his new city with epidemic and plague. Standing in the heart of the old walled city and surround by lively bazaars, the charminar ('four tower') is a 56m high triumphal arch. The arch is notable for its elegant balconies, stucco decorations and the small mosque, Hyderabad's oldest, on the 2nd floor. An image of the grace every packet of charminar cigarettes, one of India's most popular brand.

6. SANCHI STUPA

Sanchi is situated in the state of Madhya Pradesh in India. It lies at a distance of approximately 52 km from the capital city of Bhopal and 10 km from Vidisha. The major attractions of Sanchi include a number of Buddhist stupas, monasteries, temples and pillars. All these structures date back to somewhere between 3rd century BC and 12th century AD. The Mauryan emperor Ashoka founded all the stupas at Sanchi in the honor of Lord Buddha. They have the distinction of being included by UNESCO in its list of World Heritage Sites.

7. QUTAB MINAR

Qutub-ud-din Aibak laid the foundation for Qutub Minar in 1199 AD and his successor and son-in-law Shamsu'd-Din-Iitutmish completed the structure by adding three more stories. Standing at 72.5 meters, it is the highest stone tower in India. Its base diameter is 14.3 meters and its top diameter is 2.7 meters. It has 379 steps leading to its top story. The lower three stories are made using red sand stone and the top two with marble and sand stone.

8. CELLULAR JAIL

The Cellular Jail, also known as Kālā Pānī (Hindi: काला पानी कैद खाना, literally 'black water', in the sense of deep sea and hence exile), was a colonial prison situated in the

Andaman and Nicobar Islands, India. The prison was used by the British especially to exile political prisoners to the remote archipelago. Many notable freedom fighters such as Batukeshwar Dutt and Veer Savarkar, among others, were imprisoned here during the struggle for India's independence. Today, the complex serves as a national memorial monument.

9. GATEWAY

The majestic Gateway of India is a glorious historical memorial built during British rule. This magnificent monument has been built in Indo-Sarcenic style to commemorate the visit of King George V and Queen Mary to Bombay. Gateway of India is one of the finest example of colonial architectural heritage in India. This grand structure stands at the Apollo Bunder, a popular meeting place in Mumbai. The gateway of India was designed by the British architect George Wittet and was opened for general public in the year 1924.

10. VIDHAN SOUDHA

Vidhan Soudha counts amongst the most impressive as well as the most magnificent buildings in the Bangalore city of India. It is mainly famous for housing the Legislative Chambers of the state government. The three hundred rooms of Vidhan Soudha accommodate approximately twenty-two departments of the state government. The building rises to a height of almost 46 m, making it one of the most imposing structures in the city of Bangalore.

Built in the year 1956, Vidhan Soudha of Bangalore boasts of exquisite Dravidian architecture. It was built under the then chief minister of Karnataka, Mr. Kengal Hanumanthaiah, as a tribute to Indian temple architecture.

The chief engineer of Vidhan Soudha, B.R. Manickam mainly made use of granite to get the edifice constructed. In the following lines, we have provided more information on the architecture of the Vidhan Soudha of Bangalore, India.

5 Monuments and temples with the best architecture in South India

South India has some of the best monuments and temples that are architecturally brilliant. Some of these historical monuments and temples are visited both by national as well as international tourists. In South India, the temples that were constructed long back can even be classified as monuments because of their old world charm and their architectural profoundness. Let's find out the best temples and monuments that you just need to visit when you have south India on your travel agenda.

Mamallapuram Shore Temple, Chennai

Located in the Kanchipuram district, it is about 60 kms from Chennai. Being one of the oldest temples of the country and a UNESCO World Heritage site, it is also a good example of structural temples made in stone. It was in fact the first building of its time that was made of granite stone rather than rocks. It was built in the 7thcentury; this temple is a group of three temples located overlooking the Bay of Bengal in Mamallapuram. The temple is literally located on the shore, and an early morning sunrise when the sun shines through the sea onto Shiva Linga in the main shrine is a sight to behold.

Mysore Palace, Mysore

This palace belongs to the royal family of Wodeyar Maharajas. The palace you now see was redesigned and remade by an English architect in 1912. This breathtaking beautiful building has beautiful interiors and you can see different artifacts and paintings inside. One day of the week, the palace is lit with around 10000 light bulbs that make its majestic charm visible.

Meenakshi Temple, Madurai

Meenakshi temple is the temple of Parvati who is the consort of Shiva. It is also one of the few popular temples celebrating a goddess. What makes the temple so epic is the fact that it has 33000 sculptures and is the largest temple complex in the state of Tamil Nadu. The other highlight of the temple is the 14 differently made Gopurams and the thousand pillar hall that has almost 1000 pillars arranged in a fashion that they appear to be in neat rows and columns, no matter which angle you look at them from.Gopurams are pyramid shaped towers that appear mostly in the entrance of temples. It is, in fact a prominent feature of Dravidian architecture.

- wikipedia.orgCharminar, Hyderabad

Charminar is a famous mosque in the heart of Hyderabad. This place is often recommended to be the top 10 places that need to be on your travel list in India. Built in 1591 by the fifth ruler of the Qualb Shahi dynasty, it is a tourist spot that represents Islamic architecture well. Though the reason why he built it is debated, this monument is famous because of its ornate and beautiful designs. It is during winter that most people visit the mosque. It is a square structure with 20 meters each side and with four arches that face a direction that also opens into four streets. Though it is a piece of Islamic architecture, its architecture is also inspired by Hindu architecture. Many people say that the building does justice to the Hindu and Islamic cultures led by the society of Hyderabad.

Brihadeeshwarar temple, Thanjavur

Built only out of granite, this temple is one of the greatest buildings of the Chola dynasty. Located in the city of Thanjavur, it is a temple dedicated to Lord Brihadeeshwara who was an avatar (form) of Lord Shiva. The most beautiful view is the one inside the temple of Lord Shiva which is one of the biggest idols of the deity. Many say it is one of the temples that showcase Dravidian architecture brilliantly. The temple is also famous for its sculptures of various gods like Dakshinamurthi, Ganesha, Vishnu as well as "Ashta-dikpaalakas" (deities who rule the specific directions of the space) – Indra, Agni, Yama, Nirrti, Varuna, Vayu, Kubera and Isana.

Shop For This Thanjavur Temple at http://tnpoompuhar.org/tamil-nadu/pithwork/thanjavur-temple.html

This entry was posted in History, Thanjavur and tagged Thanjavur, Brihadeeshwarar temple, Hyderabad, Charminar, Madurai, Meenakshi Temple, Mysore, Mysore Palace, Shore Temple, Mamallapuram Shore Temple, architecture in South India, the best architecture in South India, the best architecture, Monuments and temples, Monuments and temples with the best architecture in South India, 5 Monuments and temples with the best architecture in South India, Chennai on February 27, 2015 by Poompuhar.

Home » In Depth » 10 Masterpieces showing Diversity in Indian Architecture

In Depth

10 Masterpieces showing Diversity in Indian Architecture

India, one of the oldest civilizations on the planet, with the most diverse cultural history and inhabited by multiple races, religions, and languages is a goldmine for the study of architectural evolution throughout history. Each transition or inclusion of new culture has created an impact on Indian architecture and art. One can easily see the different architectural styles reflecting in the buildings all over the country. This unique development of assimilating a wide variety of cultures enable us to learn how such a diverse society has evolved.

In the words of Mark Twain,"So far as I am able to judge, nothing has been left undone, either by man or nature, to make India the most extraordinary country that the sun visits on his rounds. Nothing seems to have been forgotten, nothing overlooked."

This article is just a minuscule attempt at displaying the diversity with which Indian architecture has been blessed. The following are ten most iconic yet totally independent and different architectural masterpieces having their own style of architecture. These styles have developed according to the geological conditions, cultural inclinations as well as technological advancements in their own era.

Indian Architecture: What Kind of Buildings are Popular in India?

1. Taj Mahal:

Taj Mahal- Photo:E. de Gracia Camara- Courtesy:UNESCO World Heritage Center

Taj Mahal is without a doubt, one of the most impressive pieces of architecture not only in India but all around the world. For years, it has been the face of Indian architecture for people all over the world. Built in 1653 on the orders of the Mughal ruler Shahjahan as a resting place for his beloved queen Mumtaj Mahal, it is a symbol of love. Considered to be one of the finest examples of Mughal architecture, the white marble building comprises of a square plinth having a central structure topped by a huge dome and surrounded by four minarets at each corner. It is considered as one of the seven wonders of the world in the modern era. It attracts about 3 million tourists every year thus being a hotshot for visitors globally. The Taj Mahal online website is one of the historical sites that offer free online virtual tours.

2. Lotus Temple:

Lotus Temple, Courtesy-Fariborz Sahba Architects

It is one of the modern buildings that have come up in recent times and has managed to achieve a status and fame that attracts tourists from all over the world. Conceptualized on the form of Lotus flower, it is a Bahai'i House of worship that is open to all religions and stands for the secularism and openness of the country. Designed by Iranian architect Fariborz Sahba, the structure is composed of 27 petals aligned in groupings of three thus forming a circular periphery that is co-aligned by the ritualistic beliefs of Baha'i community.

3. Amber Fort, Rajasthan:

Amber Palace- Photo:Maria J. Gutiérrez Conde-Courtesy-UNESCO World Heritage Center

Amber Fort is one of the hill forts in Rajasthan. A specimen of Hindu architecture in a Rajputana style, this fort is 11km away from the city of Jaipur. Made of Red-Sandstone and Marble, it is famous for its self-sustaining features. Having Moata Lake as its permanent water source and highly advanced ventilation system done by brilliant design, the whole structures is a prominent display of the royalty as well as the rich cultural heritage of Rajasthan.

4. Ajanta-Ellora Caves:

Ajanta & Ellora Caves- Courtesy:Archaeological Survey of India

Built during the time period of 2nd century B.C. to 6th century A.D., these caves are the finest examples of rock-cut caves. Honed out of volcanic ballistic formations while existing in a linear pattern, there are 34 caves, containing the remnants of Buddhist, Hindu and Jain temples. These walls are equipped with engravings showing the life of Lord Buddha. The purpose of these caves was to provide a sanctuary for the monks to meditate. Ellora in particular is famous for world's largest monolithic excavation leading to discovery of the great Kailasa temple.

5. Chand Baori:

Chand Baori- Photo:Ramon-Courtesy:www.chandbaori.org

It is the deepest step-well in the world. Situated in the state of Rajasthan, it was built in 9th century as a source of water for people in the neighboring villages. The whole structure is a square construction, 100 feet deep with 3500 steps and a periphery of 140 meters. It shows the geometrical intelligence of architects and local craftsmen of that era. This step-well stands as a perfect example that shows how Vernacular architecture is of, for and by the people.

6. Sun Temple, Konark:

Sun Temple- Photo:Giora Dan-Courtesy:UNESCO World Heritage Center

Lying in the coast of Bay of Bengal, it is considered one of the best examples of Dravidian Architecture. Also known as the Black Pagoda, it is considered as one of the grandest temples in India. Built in 13th century, it has a form of a giant chariot with twelve intricately crafted wheels led by seven horses. A true marvel that shows the advanced craftsmanship as well as love and devotion of that era for art.

7. Sanchi Stupa:

Sanchi Stupa- Courtesy:Archaeological Survey of India

Built in 3rd century B.C., an outstanding specimen of Buddhist art & architecture, it is one of the prominent monuments from ancient India. A stupa is generally a hemispherical dome structure containing relics of Lord Buddha. In this particular stupa, Lord Buddha has been symbolically represented by footprints, thrones, wheels etc. and all of them are exquisitely ornamented.

8. Victoria Memorial:

Victoria Memorial, Courtesy-Indiatourism.com

It is a memorial that was commemorated on the death of Queen Victoria by the Viceroy of India, Lord Curzon and opened for public in 1921. Designed by Sir William Emerson, President of the Royal Institute of British Architects, it is in a Indo-Saracenic revivalist style. According to Lord Curzon,

"Let us, therefore, have a building, stately, spacious, monumental and grand, to which every newcomer in Calcutta will turn, to which all the resident population, European and Native, will flock, where all classes will learn the lessons of history, and see revived before their eyes the marvels of the past."

Victoria Memorial, Courtesy-Indiatourism.com

Made from Makrana marbles from Rajasthan, the museum has a vast collection of remnants from the period of British Empire rule in India. Architectural elements like the great dome, clustered with four subsidiary, octagonal domed chattris, the high portals, the terrace and the domed corner towers have been used with great precision.

9. IIM Ahmedabad:

IIM Ahmedabad, Courtesy of Indian Institute of Management

Designed by American architect Louis I Kahn, it is one of the best institutional buildings in the country.This building is considered to be a great example as to how Modern architecture can seamlessly co-exist with traditional architecture, all that is needed is creativity and will. India Vernacular architecture could easily be seen in the selection of materials as well as use of geometrical compositions to give shape to something awe-inspiring. Also the stress given on not just limiting learning to classrooms therefore making spaces like hallways and plazas much more prominent. Also the use of voids in the facade of the building is one of its best features.

10. Thikse Monastery:

Thiksey Monastery- Courtesy: Vaibhav Sharma

This Buddhist monastery lies in the lap of Indus valley. Blessed by nature, it is built on a hill. The whole building is subdivided into parts according to their importance. So residents live in the lower parts while shrines are at the top. Apart from that, it is located at an altitude of 3,600 meters. Having 12-storey, it is the biggest monastery in Ladakh region. One can also find some rare and precious stupas, statues, thangkas, wall paintings and swords in the monastery. Architecturally, the most amazing features are the use of vernacular techniques in every element of buildings, whether it be walls, columns or roofs thus proving to be a great source of knowledge.

Here are the great emperors of India We took the size of the territory won and the influence on the people & culture as the measure of the emperor's greatness.

India has been the place of many rulers. Many kingdom flourished over here and they have the remains till now. Of all the kingdoms in India, there are a few kingdom which changed the scenario and history of India.

12 Greatest Kings and Warriors in Indian History !

1# Chandragupta Maurya (340 BC – 298 BC) :

He was the founder of the Maurya Empire and the first emperor to unify most of Greater India into one state. He ruled from 322 BC until his voluntary retirement and abdication in favour of his son Bindusara in 298 BC.

Chandragupta Maurya was a pivotal figure in the history of India. Prior to his consolidation of power, most of the Indian Subcontinent was divided into small states, while the Nanda Empire dominated the Indus-Gangetic Plain.[6] Chandragupta succeeded in conquering and subjugating almost all of the Indian subcontinent by the end of his reign, except the Tamil regions (Chera, Chola and Pandya) and modern day state Odisha (Kalinga). His empire extended from Bengal in the east, to Afghanistan and Balochistan in the west, to the Himalayas and Kashmir in the north, and to the Deccan Plateau in the south. It was the largest empire yet seen in Indian history

2# Ashoka Maurya (304–232 BCE) :

He was commonly known as Ashoka and Ashoka the Great, was an Indian emperor of the Maurya Dynasty who ruled almost all of the Indian subcontinent from circa 269 BCE to 232 BCE. One of India's greatest emperors, Ashoka reigned over a realm that stretched from the Hindu Kush mountains in the west to Bengal in the East and covered the entire Indian subcontinent except parts of present-day Tamil Nadu and Kerala. The empire's capital was Pataliputra (in Magadha, present-day Bihar), with provincial capitals at Taxila and Ujjain.

In about 260 BCE Ashoka waged a bitterly destructive war against the state of Kalinga (modern Odisha). He conquered Kalinga, which none of his ancestors had done.He embraced Buddhism after witnessing the mass deaths of the Kalinga War, which he himself had waged out of a desire for conquest. "Ashoka reflected on the war in Kalinga, which reportedly had resulted in more than 100,000 deaths and 150,000 deportations. Ashoka converted gradually to Buddhism beginning about 263 BCE

3# Porus a.k.a. Puru :

As for the Macedonians, however, their struggle with Porus blunted their courage and stayed their further advance into India. For having had all they could do to repulse an enemy who mustered only twenty thousand infantry and two thousand horse, they violently opposed Alexander when he insisted on crossing the river Ganges also, the width of which, as they learned, was thirty-two furlongs, its depth a hundred fathoms, while its banks on the further side were covered with multitudes of men-at-arms and horsemen and elephants. For they were told that the kings of the Ganderites and Praesii were awaiting them with eighty thousand horsemen, two hundred thousand footmen, eight thousand chariots, and six thousand fighting elephants. And there was no boasting in these reports. For Androcottus, who reigned there not long afterwards, made a present to Seleucus of five hundred elephants, and with an army of six hundred thousand men overran and subdued all India."

4# Raja Raja Chola :

He was popularly known as Raja Raja the Great (Raja Raja literally translates to 'the King of Kings'), is one of the greatest Emperors of India, who ruled between 985 and 1014 CE. He went down in history as the harbinger of the heights of Chola glory. It was during his reign that the Chola Dynasty started to emerge as a great Empire.By conquering several kingdoms in India, he expanded the Chola Empire as far as Sri Lanka in the south, and Kalinga (Odisha) in the northeast.

Raja Raja Chola was one of the greatest sovereigns of South India, a valiant conqueror and empire builder, an able administrator, a patron of arts and letters and a great builder. He was a great patron of Tamil literature as during his reign the texts of the famous Tamil poets Appar, Sambandar and Sundarar were collected and edited into one compilation called Thirumurai. He initiated a massive project of land survey and assessment in 1000 CE which strengthened the Imperial administration and which led to the reorganization of the Empire into units known as valanadus. He built the famous Brihadeeswarar Temple which is one of the largest and tallest temples in India

5# Kanishka I or Kanishka the Great:

He was the emperor of the Kushan dynasty in 127–151 famous for his military, political, and spiritual achievements.

Kanishka's empire was certainly vast. It extended from southern Uzbekistan and Tajikistan, north of the Amu Darya (Oxus) in the north west to Pakistan and Northern India, as far as Mathura in the south east (the Rabatak inscription even claims he held Pataliputra and Sri

Champa), and his territory also included Kashmir, where there was a town Kanishkapur, named after him not far from the Baramula Pass and which still contains the base of a large stupa.

6# Alha :

He was the famous general of Parmal. Why he is so special?

He fought 52 war and never lost any. He defeated The Great Ruler of Delhi Prathviraj Chauhan (many considered him as greatest). He was about to kill Prathviraj Chauhan but his Guru stopped him by saying that you are killing him only to take revenge of your brother (Udal) death, which is against the moral of a great worrier.

Originating in the Bundelkhand Region. it (Alha) recounts the intertwined fates of the three principal Rajput Kingdoms of North India on the eve of Turkish conquest (late 12th century C.E.); Delhi (ruled by Prithviraj Chauhan), Kannauj(ruled by Jaichand Rathor), and Mahoba(ruled by Chandel king Parmal). The heroes of the epic are the brothers Alha and Udal retainers of the low social status, but exceptional valour, whose cause is the protection of Mahoba and defense of its honour. Called the "Mahabarata of the Kaliyuga", Alha both parallels and inverts the themes and the structures of the classical religious epic.

7# Prithvi Raj Chauhan :

Prithviraj is considered to be the greatest warrior of India, and also one of the greatest in the world. He succeeded to the throne of Ajmer at the age of thirteen, in 1179,when his father died in a battle. His grandfather Angam, ruler of Delhi, declared him heir to the throne of Delhi after hearing about his courage and bravery. He once killed a lion on his own without any weapon. He was known as the warrior king. Chauhan was the last independent Hindu king, before Hemu, to sit upon the throne of Delhi. He succeeded to the throne in 1169 CE at the age of 20, and ruled from the twin capitals of Ajmer and Delhi.

He defeated the mighty Bheemdev, ruler of Gujarat, at the mere age of thirteen. He was trained in Archery and could aim at target while being blind folded (Shabdabhedi Ban Vidya).

His love story with his enemy, Jaichand's daughter, Samyukta/Sanyogita is very famous. He rode off with her on the day of her 'Swayamwara'.

8# Hemu a.k.a. Hemchandra Vikramaditya :

Hemu (died 5 November 1556) was a Hindu emperor of North India during the 16th century CE, a period when the Mughals and Afghans were vying for power in the region.

Hemu acceded to the throne of Delhi on 7 October 1556 after defeating Akbar's Mughal forces in the Battle of Delhi in the Tughlakabad area in Delhi, and became the de facto king assuming the title of Vikramaditya that had been adopted by many Hindu kings since Vedic times.[3] He re-established native rule (albeit for a short duration) in North India, after over 350 years of Turkish and Mughal rule.

9# Maharana Pratap :

He was a Hindu rajput ruler of Mewar Kingdom.

Nearly all of Pratap's fellow Rajput chiefs had meanwhile entered into the vassalage of the Mughals. Even

Pratap's own brothers, Shakti Singh and Sagar Singh, served Akbar. Indeed, many Rajput chiefs, such as Raja Man Singh of Amber (later known as Maharaja of Jaipur) served as army commanders in Akbar's armies and as members of his council.

Akbar sent a total of six diplomatic missions to Pratap, seeking to negotiate the same sort of peaceful alliance that he had concluded with the other Rajput chiefs. Each time, however, Pratap politely refused to accept Akbar's suzerainty, arguing that the Sisodia Rajputs had never accepted any foreign ruler as their overlord, nor will he. It is worth noting that both these rulers' grandfathers, Rana Sanga and Babur, had previously fought against each other. Thus the enmity was not only political, but was also a bit personal.

Pratap maintained that he had no intention to fight with Akbar but he could not bow down to Akbar and accept him as the ruler. Some scholars argue that there was some possibility that Maharana could have become friends with Akbar but in the siege of Chittor when Akbar killed 30,000 civilian, unarmed residents of Chittor, because they refused to convert to Islam, left a lasting impression on Maharana's mind and he decided he cannot bow to such an unjust and cruel human being as Akbar was.

10# Shivaji (1674–1680 CE) :

He established a competent and progressive civil rule with the help of a disciplined military and well-structured administrative organisations. He innovated military tactics, pioneering the guerrilla warfare methods (Shiva sutra or ganimi kava), which leveraged strategic factors like geography, speed, and surprise and focused pinpoint attacks to defeat his larger and more powerful enemies. From a small contingent of 2,000 soldiers inherited from his father, Shivaji created a force of 100,000 soldiers; he built and restored strategically located forts both inland and coastal to safeguard his territory. He revived ancient Hindu political traditions and court conventions and promoted the usage of Marathi and Sanskrit, rather than Persian, in court and administration.

Shivaji he is the greatest king and most successful general in Indian history; he is the father of Indian navy nobody else recognised the importance of a navy except him. he is the first general in Indian history to have used the geographical terrain to his advantage. he kept the dream of swaraj (self rule) above everything else; his successful military adventures; his escape from Agra; his escape to vishalgad; his military expeditions in karnataka are legends moreover he was a very inspiring general almost none of his cheiftains ever decieved him. also he was inspired by king bali this theological character is said to have established a kingdom of farmers; shivaji was a very kind ruler. he established laws that were responsible for social integrity of state. he even established mosque on raigad for muslim slodiers. cases against women were dealt with death penalty.

11# Maharaja Ranjit Singh :

The founder of the Sikh empire ,A man who had lost one eye, an arm, and yet built one of the greatest empires in India. He drove out the Durranis from Punjab, captured Multan, Peshawar, annexed the whole pf Punjab. His kingdom extended right up to the foothills of the Sulaiman Mountains, and conquered Kasur from the fierce Pathans. His empire consisted of undivided Punjab(extending till Multan now in Pakistan), Jammu and Kashmir till Gilgit now in POK, North West frontier till Khyber Pass and even parts of Western Tibet. And he had some formidable generals like Hari Singh Nalwa, Dewan Mokham Chand, Zorawar Singh along with Europeans like Jean Francois Allard.

12# TIPU Sultan :

Won small battles against British with 1:1 forces, while suffering small losses before he was 30. He was crown prince at the time. became King with a proven track record.

The last Indian King to dictate terms to the British after defeating them in battle.

Lord Charles Cornwallis, after mixed results in American war of Independence thought that he can improve his military record by coming to India. What a miscalculation a battle against Tipu turned out to be Tipu practically invented usage of rockets in warfare. They were present during his fathers time, but Tipu refined it for use in battle. The rockets were inefficient by modern terms, but they were meant for chaos and commotion to disperse the enemy.

Tipu had a good laugh after unleashing his rocket infantry: Tipu was cruel and not a worthy King because of how he treated his prisoners and humiliation of defeated enemies. But as a warrior, he is unparalleled and is the Indian equivalent of "Last Samurai" as he was the last king to defeat the British at battle. That makes him a strong contender for this title.